MAN UP

JUSTIN KAVANAUGH

This book is dedicated to every athlete that takes the time to read it and invest into their life. I want to see you achieve greatness.

Acknowledgements

This book would not have been anything but ideas in my head and bullet points on a sticky note if it weren't for Cody Journell. The idea came to me on my trip with my wife, Tanya, to Barcelona. Our guide on one of our tours said "you don't have the Balls to bet an old Spaniard", so I called him out. I came back with two pages of barely legible, scrambled thoughts that Cody took from scratch and we turned them into what you are reading now. We had a few too many lunches at Santini's and late night edits, but you made this into something I am proud of. Because of your help, I can hold true to my word and deliver. Thanks Cody, it has been fun to write this with you and see you grow into a pro athlete and a coach yourself.

I would also like to thank everyone that has affected me in my life and career. It is from those interactions that I learned and became the man I am today. This book started as a bet from Dr. Ken Kinakin and me giving him my word that I would finish it. I got pestered by Dr. Serrano everyday that it wasn't out, and I am thankful for them as mentors and friends who push me. To Charlie, Austin and Jen who helped edit and put their insights into this book, Matt Shaner for your help in editing and layout: you helped shape it into what it is and I am very thankful for your time.

Intro

"Character strong as steel
won't develop with skin smooth as silk"
- Coach Kav

I grew up in an era where coaches, parents and elders showed they cared about you by being hard on you, testing you, and pushing you beyond what you thought was capable or achievable. Because of this, I became not only a better football, soccer, and baseball player, but also a better man.

I played absolutely everything I could get my hands on—from a ball to a puck and even throwing on the gloves. The importance of playing everything I could possibly fit into my schedule wasn't the fact that it made me a better all-around athlete (although it certainly did). The true value was found in my exposure to so many different coaches and coaching styles.

The great coaches were always the ones who got my attention right away. Some were extremely intense and in your face. Others just had to give you "the look" and that would completely destroy you. But they all had a way of pushing me past my comfort zone, and most importantly, teaching me about myself and how to apply the things I learned beyond the field; outside of the game.

Like any stubborn kid growing up (which is putting things lightly), I didn't view my coaches and elders being as influential in my life as they actually were. With their toughness, experience, and persistence, they molded me into the man I am today. I didn't recognize that fact and importance until much later in life when I was able to better grasp the concepts they were drilling into my brain. I still work on these principles in my own life today.

Now, I believe we have a problem in our country.

You may look around and notice there aren't as many influential coaches molding youth, and you might think it's a coaching problem. However, I believe it's a generation problem.

You are being raised in an environment in which everyone gets a trophy. Parents say things like, "How dare you raise your voice to my kid and possibly hurt his feelings." or, "Everyone should get equal playing time no matter what." How can any coach demand and enforce a certain standard while trying to abide by these societal guidelines? All this fluffy stuff is turning you into just that, FLUFF. Is that what you want? The minute we stop allowing you to be strongly coached, we remove the pressure that's needed to form the diamond you have potential to be.

America has become soft.

Children are soft. Our leaders are soft. We are losing the very grit that built this great nation. We've become so soft that praying and standing for the national anthem offends people. We're too small-minded and too caught up in our own insecurities to see the bigger picture.

Instead of putting on my cape and trying to shift an entire culture to adopt my ideology (which is near impossible), I believe we need to start with you. All those who have ever achieved greatness did so because they wanted to. There is no accident in greatness. If you want it, find a way to get it. You need pressure as a young man, so when you are faced with a real-life situation you are strong enough to handle it.

Take a hard look at yourself and see if you are doing things every day to become your best. How bad do you want it? Do you have what it takes?

Be honest and MAN UP.

Prelude

"Yo have no huevous."

Initially, I wanted to title this book *Grow Some BALLS!* And as passionately as I felt about the suggestion, I was strongly advised to reconsider. After the first push-back, I thought: *I can't cave on this.* I mean that is the whole premise of the book—to be strong-willed and stand for what you believe in whether it hurts someone's feelings or not. But when I realized that "grow some balls" was just a way of saying MAN UP and do the right thing, that's when it clicked.

No matter what you want in life it all starts with *why*. My *what* is to MAN UP. But being the best husband, father, coach and mentor I possibly can, representing God, and being my best every day—that is my significance and purpose. That is my *why*.

Now I know the first thing that may come to mind when you hear *balls* is what's between your legs. However, I urge you to take a different look. For this book, *balls* represents so much more than that. It stands for everything you need in order to achieve your end goal: to be better at life and in your sport. To break it down, BALLS is an acronym:

B = Balance
A = Accountability
L = Lust
L = Love
S = Sacrifice

When you understand and master these concepts, there is no doubt you will reap the athletic rewards. By sharing my personal experiences as an athlete and a coach, as well as experiences from leaders, professionals, and businessmen who mastered (or failed to master) these concepts, growing some BALLS will prove to be the key for you to MAN UP.

After you determine your goal and what you want to accomplish, the next step is to identify what priorities must be in place to make it happen. Finding the equilibrium of the right things will propel you closer to your end goal, and when you master this you will have balance.

Ask yourself:
Do I want to achieve my goal so badly that I am willing to put up with people or coaches that I may dislike? Trust me this will happen. But, not liking them shouldn't be an excuse to give up, so long as they hold you accountable for the things you're supposed to be doing to accomplish your dream.

Do I want what I'm chasing after so badly that I'm willing to push through anything that may get in my way? Do I lust for the achievement of knowing that if I had this certain thing it would make me feel a certain way?

You should be excited every day to chase your dream; knowing that if you accomplished it and experienced the feeling of standing on the highest podium, it would all be worth it.

Is the feeling I get when my parents stand proud watching me succeed something I love?

Maybe it is. Or maybe you love the competition, and that's what keeps you going. Regardless, your answers are why you are doing it.

As you look at all the things you want to do or accomplish, you also need to look at what you are willing to sacrifice. You then must be willing to ask yourself an even more important question:

Do I have what it takes to actually get what I want?

If you're truly honest with yourself and at the moment the answer is no, that's OK; you will get there. But knowing that you really want something, especially if it's an ambitious goal, requires you to ask yourself if you have what it takes to succeed. You can either let things happen, or make them happen.

"*Remember, it's draft day, not draft career.*"
-Hugh Freeze

When I think of what it means to be a man, to have *BALLS,* I think of my father. My father was multi-sport athlete, and hands down one of the best coaches I ever had. But it was his career as Captain of the City of Hialeah Fire Department (one of the most diverse areas in Miami) that I first witnessed him command a group of men and women. At the time I couldn't understand why they viewed him as such an authoritative figure (I mean, he was "just dad" to me). But as I matured I started to understand why.

I remember visiting the firehouse and seeing the crew playing basketball, making jokes, and enjoying meals together. But when the bell rang they all snapped into work mode. They would jump into their boots, grab their bunker gear and pile into the truck (a sight I often got used to during visits).

In sports, you often find yourself at practice or training screwing around having fun. Then a coach snaps for, seemingly, no apparent reason. If you don't jump back in line just like the guys getting on the truck to fight a fire, you reap the consequences. This may simply be extra conditioning at practice, or it may be much worse. But if you don't learn how to dial it in, eventually it could end up costing you a game, or an entire season.

It is very important that each fire department work as a unit, and each person within that unit must play their role accordingly. The fire department is very similar to a sports team, but in their "game," people's lives (including their own) are at stake. When the department receives an emergency call, there is trust that every team member will be accountable in all phases of the job—being timely in response to the bell, accuracy in delivery, and precision in execution. In order for this to culminate into a successful end result, each person must accomplish exactly what their job requires. One weak link will make the whole chain useless.

It's a very interesting dynamic within the duty of a firefighter. Most people don't understand that someone actually enjoys putting their life on the line for work. Firefighters *lust* after something that is very dangerous: the call to a large fire. It's something that every firefighter you will ever talk to has in common. They can't help but get excited every time they hear the bell. That passion is something that's engrained deep down in their soul, and there's no taking it away from them. I felt the same way about football. Friday nights in high school and the Saturday games I looked forward to all week in college were almost like a drug to me. I licked my chops all week just dreaming of kickoff time. I would be able to step onto the field and sacrifice my body for my teammates and the crowd. No one could take that feeling away from me. That's lust. For my father, responding to an emergency or being in a split-second decision between pumping, breaking, or entering a situation that was life threatening was a thrill that he lusted for.

Yet, as much as firefighters enjoy the risk and responsibility of what they do, there is nothing they love more than the drive home from a

24-hour shift to see their families. It's what gives them the energy to keep working even when in a tough situation. When the calls don't go their way, they don't enjoy their day to say the least.

Trust me, I remember the look on my father's face when he came home from a bad one. I could see in his eyes he was carrying an internal load that was almost too heavy to bare. But I also remember that every time he saw us, the load lifted a little.

The love for family keeps firefighters doing their job, provides food for the table, and creates opportunity for the future. That is their *why*.

Sometimes, when pursuing something in life, it's not enough to get through everything with just lust. They have an amazing ability to sacrifice their lives day in and day out to save others while knowing their own families are waiting for them to come home unharmed. That is the ultimate form of selflessness in my eyes. That is the ultimate form of love.

"Greater love hath no man than this, that a man lay down his life for another."
-John 15:13

BALANCE

ACCOUNTABILITY

LUST

LOVE

SACRIFICE

Balance

"The calm and balanced mind is the strong and great mind; the hurried and agitated mind is the weak one."
-Wallace D. Wattles

Being a man requires having strategic priorities in your life and knowing where they lie. My top priorities have always been God, Family, School, and Sports—in that order. Although the last two frequently switched around, I gave no time to anything disruptive that tried to come between my top priorities. I saw those disruptions as immediate threats or distractions to what my end goal was as an athlete.

Don't get me wrong, the social and dating aspects of your early life are very important in how you handle yourself as you get older. There are many lessons that come from interacting with peers and learning how to be in relationships that carry over into your specific sport. But it is evident in high school, collegiate, and even professional athletes who let disruptions get in the way, that they didn't take the time to make sure they had BALANCE

The Greatest Have BALANCE.

Take Tiger Woods' life for example. Early in his career some would say Tiger had it all: Nike endorsements, millions of dollars, even his own video game (not to mention the 79 PGA Tour events, 14 Majors, and 4 Green Jackets he's won). But in 2009, it all came crashing down. From the time Tiger was a young boy, his father Earl molded and groomed him into a fine young man and an outstanding golfer. After serving two tours of duty in Vietnam as a U.S. Army Infantry Officer, Earl retired and played golf every day—holding his club's lowest handicap at the age of 42 (of course until his son came along). As an Army Officer, Earl instilled principles in Tiger at a young age that helped propel his son to greatness. But when his father died on May 3, 2006, Tiger's world turned upside down. The balance of his life was off tilt. He lost sight of what was most important in his life and career—golf and his family.

On Thanksgiving night in 2009, Tiger's image was shattered in a single incident.

He crashed his car into a fire hydrant while attempting to run from his irate wife after finding evidence of his affair with another woman. Turned out it was multiple women. This led to the demise of his image and has affected his career to this day. He lost his sponsorships, his swing, and even his family.

In more ways than one, Tiger's life was off balance. He was making things priorities that weren't helping him reach his end goal of surpassing Jack Nicklaus's record of 6 Green Jackets—something that's looking more and more out of reach.

Of course losing someone so close and so influential to you is devastating, and I'm not faulting Tiger for making mistakes after such a tragedy—he is only human, and we are all bound to make mistakes in life. But even he would agree his story is an example of what could happen when your priorities, balance, and synergy don't match up with your end goal.

"Man maintains his balance, poise,
and sense of security only as he is moving forward."
-Maxwell Maltz

Peyton Manning's career also proves the power and importance of proper balance. This is a guy who is arguably the greatest quarterback to ever pick up a football. Despite his impressive stats and on field achievements, the most impressive part of Peyton's career is how he was able to balance the demanding schedule of an elite NFL quarterback while giving his wife and kids the attention that they deserved.

There's a lot that goes into being a professional athlete, especially as a quarterback in the NFL. It takes a well-balanced person to learn how to deal with the long practice schedule, studying hours of film in preparation for the next opponent, staying in shape to prevent injury, coping with the media, and so on. But in order to become the best in the world, Peyton realized early in his career that these things needed to be done—he now has 5 NFL MVP Awards and 2 Super Bowl Rings to show for it.

From the ages of 15 to 35, Peyton never missed a game due to injury.

That is a remarkable stat if you stop and think about how many times he's been knocked around as a quarterback over that twenty year period. In 2011, Peyton had a neck injury that finally sidelined him. The injury required 4 surgeries to get him back to playing condition, and in that time Manning said he realized something: He's not a robot. He needed to change his preparation routine late in his career.

"There was a time when I could come home from practice, and I would stay up until 1:30 in the morning watching all four of the exhibition games that night. I thought if I didn't the world might come to an end the next day. I didn't need to sleep as much as a younger player. But now I come home, and I love spending time with the kids and putting them to bed. I don't stay up as late. I need to get my rest more."

Peyton recognized the importance balance plays in performing at an elite level in his sport. He realized that excess in one area leads to destruction in another. And that's what creating balance as a man is all about. Sometimes you need to do the things that you don't want to, or make certain things a priority that you know aren't as important. It's putting your head down or your ego aside to get things done, because you know achieving that balance takes you closer to your end goal. For Peyton, his reward was winning another Super Bowl.

"A successful man is one who can lay a firm foundation with the bricks others have thrown at him."
-David Brinkley

For the majority of the journey for any athlete, they are playing their sport and putting in the time of a full time job for no pay. I was in the same boat when I played. Early in high school, I couldn't get a regular job due to my schedule packed with practice and games. I always enjoyed music growing up, so I picked up DJing on the weekends. It was an opportunity to work my own schedule and make money while staying focused on my priorities. It was my way of balancing what I wanted and what I needed in order to work with the situation I was in.

As an athlete, you can either complain about your situation or do something about it. I needed to go to class so I could play ball after school, and I wanted to make money so I found a work around my schedule. That's what I mean by balance.

Let's take a look at one of the greatest ever to step into the rap game, Sean Carter. You know him best by the name, Jay-Z. He's one of the most successful hip-hop artists in history, growing from a rapper to now businessman and investor. With a career that began in 1989, Jay-Z grew his net worth to an estimated $520 million in just under eighteen years. It's no secret that he started his life off on the streets of Brooklyn as a hustler, but his raw talent, love for music, and vision for a successful future enabled him to leave the streets and enter into the music industry.

I'm sure you are aware by now that Jay-Z is not just an artist, but is also a genuine business kingpin. Some of his most successful business ventures include: Roc Nation, The New Jersey Nets, The 40/40 Club, Rocawear, and Tidal, just to name a few.

All while churning out more Billboard 200 albums than any other solo artist (and any group outside The Beatles). He's won ten Grammy awards and sold forty-five million albums worldwide, all while raising a family with one of the most successful women in the world, Beyoncé.

That's a lot for any man to achieve in lifetime, let alone in less than two decades. But what do you think is the most important attribute to his success? No doubt the guy has talent, but we see talented people come and go in every industry without seeing the success Jay-Z has had. The answer is balance.

Jay-Z strategically determines what priorities are going to launch him to the next level of success, and then he reorganizes his priorities in order to make it happen. While hustling on the streets of Brooklyn, he knew there was more to life than having an apartment, a nice car, nice clothes, and being able to provide for himself.

He saw beyond that; he saw the big picture of where he wanted to be and decided to leave that part of his life behind to focus on music.

Throughout his career, Jay-Z notoriously separates himself from people once he outgrows them or feels held back by the relationship. His first partner, JazO, bought a sound mixer and taught Jay-Z the ins and outs of programming and how to put together a song. JazO basically took him out of the projects and gave him his first taste of the music industry. But Jay-Z ultimately left him behind because he didn't feel he was pulling his weight anymore.

Another partner, Damon Dash, who was perhaps most integral to Jay-Z's success, started trying things that didn't align with Jay-Z's vision. He eventually parted ways with Dash too. Jay-Z seeks to identify with those who have the knowledge he wants to acquire. Repeatedly throughout his career, he absorbs his mentor's abilities, surpasses them, and leaves them behind.

You might consider this a negative, like he isn't giving proper credit where it's due. I think it's genius. It reminds me of famed actor and martial artist Bruce Lee's principle: Absorb what is useful, reject what is useless. Jay-Z knows the importance of balance, but recognizes another component of what it takes to MAN UP. He knows if his partners aren't accountable or holding him accountable, they are holding him back.

"We can be sure that the greatest hope for maintaining equilibrium in the face of any situation rests within ourselves."
-Francis J. Braceland

BALANCE

1. _____
2. _____
3. _____
4. _____
5. _____

WHY IS EACH A PRIORITY TO YOU?

1. _____
2. _____
3. _____
4. _____
5. _____

LOOK AT THE FIRST TWO PRIORITIES. WOULD YOUR FIRST TWO BE PROUD OF YOU SPENDING THE REST OF YOUR TIME ON #'S 3, 4, & 5?

HOW MANY HOURS A WEEK DO YOU SPEND ON 3, 4 AND 5?

3. _____

4. _____

5. _____

NOTE:

TAKE A LOOK AT HOW MUCH TIME YOU SPEND ON EACH PRIORITY. DOES THE TIME SPENT MATCH THE PRIORITY RANK? IF NOT, DO YOU THINK YOU SHOULD REARRANGE THE LEVEL OF PRIORITY? OR DO YOU NEED TO REFOCUS YOUR TIME TOWARDS WHAT'S MORE IMPORTANT?

FOR EXAMPLE, IF GOD AND FAMILY ARE YOUR FIRST 2 PRIORITIES, THEN THOSE SHOULD BE THE THINGS THAT YOU HONESTLY THINK REPRESENT YOU AS A PERSON. IF THEY ARE NOT YOUR TOP TWO PRIORITIES, BUT THAT'S HOW YOU WANT TO REPRESENT YOURSELF. THEN YOU NEED TO CHANGE SOME THINGS IN YOUR LIFE IN ORDER TO RE-PRIORITIZE.

BALANCE

ACCOUNTABILITY

LUST

LOVE

SACRIFICE

Accountability

"When your teammate looks you in the eye and holds you accountable, that's the greatest kind of leadership there is."
-Doug Collins, Philadelphia 76ers Coach

ACCOUNTABILITY is the foundation of trust.

In any sport, but most particularly in team sports, trust is the driving factor to any team's success. Players must be able to trust that each teammate will take care of his specific job. They must trust that the coach has the game plan together so they can follow his orders to victory. And the coach must trust that the players are willing to give their maximum effort to win the game. If even one person is not accountable for their duty, they either fail as a team, or someone else has to pick up the slack.

Accountability is being ready to do your job, no matter what your role on the team is. Even if you're the last man on the bench, you need to be prepared to come in and contribute because you never know when your number is going to be called.

Look back at Super Bowl XLII between the New England Patriots, who were looking to cap off an undefeated season, and the heavy-underdog New York Giants. Few people thought the Giants would win. If you asked those few who would play a key role in a Giants victory, none of them would have said David Tyree.

Most of the world didn't even know who Tyree was. He served as a backup receiver on the team and was known primarily for his work on special teams. He finished his career with just 54 catches and only had four catches for 35 yards during the 2007 season. Those don't sound like the numbers a Super Bowl hero would put up. There's also a famous story about how he struggled in a practice he had a few days before the Big Game and couldn't catch anything.

"I probably approached him just to let him know, 'Hey man, you know I'll be ready,'" Tyree said in an ESPN.com article about a talk he had with Eli Manning during the practice. "And even before I could finish my sentence, he said, 'Don't worry about none of that. You know I'm coming for you.'"

Tyree kept his word as he caught his first touchdown of the season on a 5-yard pass with 11:05 left in the fourth quarter to give the Giants a 10-7 lead. However, in typical Patriots fashion, New England drove 80 yards on 12 plays to take a 17-14 lead with 2:42 left in the game when Tom Brady hit Randy Moss with a 6-yard TD pass. Most would assume, and understandably so, that the TD catch earlier in the quarter would be Tyree's only highlight of the game, and that the Patriots would put the finishing touches on the greatest season in NFL history. Little did we know, Tyree and Manning were about to shock the world.

Manning got the ball back and moved the Giants down the field. He picked up two first downs, but a short run and an incomplete pass made it 3rd and 5 on the Giants' 44-yard line. With the Super Bowl on the line, Offensive Coordinator Kevin Gilbride called the play "Phantom," later to be headlined around the world as "The Catch". As the ball was snapped, the pocket started collapsing. Not the most mobile quarterback, Eli did everything he could to avoid a sack. Even with an opposing defensive linemen gripping his jersey, Eli was able to wiggle free. Like any great quarterback, he kept his eyes down the field. Tyree broke off his route and pulled up to give Eli a shot. And Eli took it.

"We've got him sacked," Harrison said. "He throws a Hail Mary. And I thought for sure it was incomplete." But little did he know David

Tyree, with possibly the shortest vertical jump ability on the team (30 inches), would get to his highest point over Harrison and pin the ball on the top of his helmet. The catch would keep the Giants' drive alive and a Super Bowl victory still within reach. Three plays later, Manning hit Steve Smith with a 12-yard pass for a first down. Then he threw a touchdown to Plaxico Burress, putting the Giants up 17-14 with 35 seconds left—not enough time for even back-to-back MVP Tom Brady to drive down the field and score.

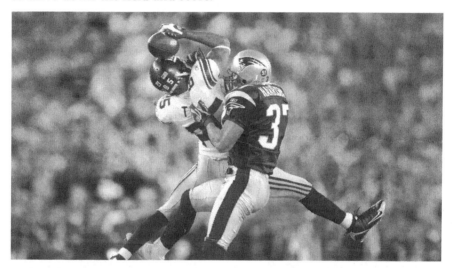

www.si.com/specials/100-greatest/?q=19-the-helmet-catch

I truly believe the only reason Tyree was able to make the catch was in that singular moment, where time stood still and he was fully extended in the air with a ball pinned to his helmet, every person on that team was doing exactly what they were supposed to do.

The offensive coordinator called a great play. The O-Line held off the defense just long enough to let Eli slip through and find his target down field. The other receivers ran their routes with intent, pulling the secondary away from the point of the catch. David Tyree broke his route off early noticing Eli was in trouble, and he was able to get a half second open in order to make the catch (not mentioning the great defense they played against it). But that's what being accountable is all about. All of that led to arguably the greatest catch in Super Bowl history.

The true lesson is that everyone had a responsibility and they took care of their job. Everyone on the field trusted their teammates would do their job so that they could do their own. A team's ability to have everyone play a role throughout the process, and hold themselves and each other accountable, makes champions.

I tell my athletes the team is their ship. They control it, and anyone in the boat not pulling their weight should be gone. Life is the same way. Have a small core group of people who support your dreams. If they don't, get rid of them.

While on the New England Patriots, five time Pro Bowler and first round draft pick Vince Wilfork said,

"Everybody is going to have to be accountable. If you're on the field, you have to give me 100 percent. Always. We have to weed out the bad seeds, point blank. If you can't give me what I'm giving you on the field, I don't need you on the field with me. I have no problem telling that guy I don't need him on the field, and I have no problem going to tell Bill (Belichick) I don't want him on the field. That's how you win."

That's what it takes to be a man and a champion. I don't give a damn about hurting someone's feelings. You and I are both here for one reason and one reason only; to win. If you aren't pulling your weight, or I'm not pulling mine, I fully expect someone to call it out. If you look at 99% (maybe 100% even) of the teams that won a championship, they all held each other accountable. No dancing around feelings or formalities.

They would look their teammate in the eye and tell them point blank, "You need to get better at this, try harder, or focus more in order for us to succeed as a team."

"On good teams coaches hold players accountable, on great teams players hold players accountable."
-Joe Dumars, Detroit Pistons

I have had a lot of people in my corner over the years and the most important factor in knowing someone has your back is trust and accountability. You can't have one without the other.

Bryan Millan is one of those guys I would completely trust with my life. Why? Not because he played on James Madison University's National Championship football team. Not because he interned and coached for me. But because he served 8 years in the Army. The U.S. Military is the most powerful force in the world. We have the best trained men and women, and they are consistently victorious in all aspects of battle. Accountability is at the core of training across each military branch. From the highest rank to the lowest enlistee, each person has a job to do, and is held accountable for that specific job.

Possibly the most elite of these branches, and certainly the most respected, are the Navy SEALS. You may think these guys are crazy for entering a smoke filled room littered with enemies pointing weapons at them. The SEALS do it without hesitation because they trust their teammates. They are like a well-oiled machine. In order for it to run smoothly each piece must function correctly. When entering a room, the front man can't do his job (clear the left side of the room) unless he has complete trust that the guy coming in behind him will clear the right side of the room. These missions require a tremendous amount of discipline for the lead man and trust in the second man.

Without trust, there is no SEAL team.

Consider the story in the book, *No Easy Day,* by Mark Owen from SEAL Team Six. Owen highlights the training and objectives that led up to his team being part of the final mission that killed Osama Bin Laden. Mark recalled a mission they had in Afghanistan's mountainous Kunar Province. That night, their objective was for him and his eight-person team to conduct a kill-or-capture operation on high-level Taliban.

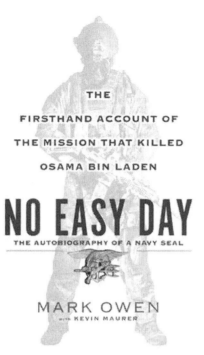

He wrote, "The alley was narrow, and my partner and I stood on opposite walls. Instinctively I covered his side of the wall with my laser and I could see his laser in front of me. We crept down the alley, being as quiet as possible. We'd go fast when needed, but then go back to being slow and quiet. We were about halfway down the alley when I heard pop, pop, pop! I froze in my tracks, I couldn't see what was in front of me. My partner had let loose a short burst and then started to move forward [as if nothing happened]. I glanced ahead for a split second and saw a fighter crumple to the ground holding a shotgun pointed at me...he had been less than 3 feet in front of me."

Whoa, talk about trusting someone to be accountable. If Mark's partner hadn't done his job, what would have been the outcome? A failed mission? A dead teammate? Probably both.

This example of an extreme situation holds true to all aspects of sports and life. We must be accountable for our own responsibilities. If you aren't doing what's required of you, how can you expect someone else to be accountable for their job? MAN UP and do what you're supposed to do! Check off the boxes required to get the final result.

"Responsibility equals accountability equals ownership. And a sense of ownership is the most powerful weapon a team or organization can have."
-Pat Summitt, Former Tennessee Women's Basketball Coach

ACCOUNTABILITY

WHAT ARE 5 THINGS YOU HOLD YOURSELF ACCOUNTABLE FOR?

1. _____
2. _____
3. _____
4. _____
5. _____

NAME 3 PEOPLE YOU HOLD ACCOUNTABLE.

1. _____
2. _____
3. _____

NAME 3 PEOPLE THAT HOLD YOU ACCOUNTABLE.

1. _____
2. _____
3. _____

DESCRIBE A TIME WHEN YOU HELD YOURSELF ACCOUNTABLE FOR ONE OF YOUR 5 THINGS. WHAT ENDED UP BEING THE RESULT OF DOING SO?

_____

_____

_____

DESCRIBE A TIME WHEN YOU HELD SOMEONE ELSE ACCOUNTABLE. WHAT COULD HAVE BEEN THE RESULT IF YOU DIDN'T HOLD THEM TO THEIR RESPONSIBILITY?

_____

_____

_____

WHAT ARE THREE THINGS YOU COULD TO HOLD YOURSELF MORE ACCOUNTABLE TOWARDS YOUR GOALS?

1. _____

2. _____

3. _____

BALANCE

ACCOUNTABILITY

LUST

LOVE

SACRIFICE

Lust

"The starting point of all achievement is desire."
-Napoleon Hill

LUST is defined as a strong sexual desire or a very strong passion for something. Lust can give you an initial push or drive to accomplish something. I'm sure you've heard your parents and peers talk about lust as it relates to relationships.

This is typically a negative conversation. I, however, challenge you to view this word as another positive. It's like when your father tells you lifting weights will help you with your sport and make you a man. You never listen. You always get to it later, or at best half-ass the workout if he drug you to the gym.

Then one day you meet a girl and she gives you one ounce of interest. You think, *Oh shit. I better get after it in the gym and show her what I'm made of.* You put the time in and see the results begin to manifest in your body quickly. You start noticing bigger biceps and the start of a barreled chest like Arnold (you think).

Your lust triggered action and improvement.

Lusting after something indicates an extreme passion for it. Remember my father and the way he and his crew felt about putting out fires? You could really feel the passion they put into their work. When you find the right things in life you're truly passionate about, those things are going to springboard you toward success.

*"I have put my heart and my soul into my work,
and have lost my mind in the process."*
-Vincent Van Gogh

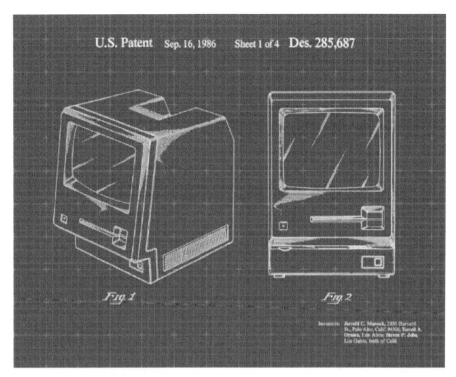

www.printapatent.com/Technology/i-fjw8Mvr

If you are living in the US and own a smartphone, there's roughly a 66.9% chance that if you looked down right now you're holding some version of an iPhone. Apple opened shop in 1976 and from that day forward changed how people used and viewed technology. Largely in part to the mastermind Steve Jobs. Unfortunately, Steve died on October 5, 2011. But not before he changed the world we live and interact in today.

It's safe to say he was a genius—certainly one of the most influential people of our time. Steve was a very driven person, and it's easy to see how he was able to do so much in such a short period of time. It was also easy to see that Steve didn't have any lack of lust in his life. Lust for his company. Lust for his products. Lust for his own self. This overabundance of lust caused him to lose many friends, create a number of enemies, and probably burn his share of bridges.

Yet again, lust doesn't always have to be a negative thing. In fact, lust inspires creativity. It's what makes that fire inside of us burn.

For Jobs, it was his lust that inspired his innovation. Regardless of how he handled his relationships (although later in life he admitted he regretted the way that he treated a lot of people), this drive propelled Apple and the technology industry to what it is today.

His original business partner, Steve Waz, said in an interview after his death, " [Jobs] had an ability to think out new ways of doing things. Not just ways to improve what we have, or do a better version of something, but do it in a totally different way that the world would swing towards. He had this crazy knack for seeing into the future of what people want and was willing to risk it all to propel the world in that direction."

I remember hearing him explain his views on the restrictions modern day society puts on us and how we think. It takes a special person to think beyond the status quo, and even moreso apply these thoughts towards action.

Jobs said,

"When you grow up you tend to be told the world is the way it is. And your life is just to live your life inside the box, try not to bash into the walls too much. Try to have a nice family life, have fun, save a little money. But that's a very limited life. **Life can be much broader once you discover one simple fact. And that is, everything around you that you call life was made up by people that were no smarter than you. The moment that you understand that if you poke life, if you push in and something else will pop out the other side. When you understand that you can change it, you can mold it. That's the most important thing. And once you learn that you will never be the same again.**"

"The will to win, the desire to succeed, the urge to reach your full potential... these are the keys that will unlock the door to personal excellence."
-Confucius

In 1954, if you walked down South Fourth Street in Louisville on a particular fall morning, you could catch a glimpse of a 12-year-old Cassius Clay sitting on the steps of Columbia Auditorium angry and crying. Someone stole his bike. Clay was so furious about the incident that he sought out Joe Martin, a police officer at the time, and reported his bike stolen. Joe Martin recalled little Clay telling him, "If I find who stole my bike, I'm gonna whoop him." What Clay didn't know at the time was that Joe was also a part time boxing trainer.

Joe Martin asked string bean thin Clay, "Do you know how to fight? You should know how to fight if you're going to whoop somebody."

That's all it took. The next night young Cassius Clay met Joe at his gym and he came back night after night. With the memory of whoever took his bike fresh in his mind, each hit at the heavy bag was fueled by the thought of what he was going to do to the thief once he was found.

He trained until after a while it wasn't even about the bike anymore.

Clay found something that lit a fire inside of him. At this point he was in the gym 6 days a week, waking up early to run each morning. In the evenings he trained at the gym with Joe for several hours, working on his technique and endurance. When Joe's gym closed, he walked to another gym to continue training.

One small incident spurred a 12-year-old boy to start boxing. At first, all that drove him was the hatred for the kid who stole his bike. He was going to do everything he could to make sure he could "whoop" whoever it was that stole his most prized possession. But after a while, the initial lust wore off and he found something that he loved, boxing.

Clay later changed his name to Muhammad Ali, and new things drove him to become better and better—in this case, to be the best in the world. If you look back in the history books of sports and read about some of the greatest athletes to have ever played, there's a similarity between many of them (if not almost all of them). There was an initial reason for starting what they are now famous for doing. More often than not it's not the same reason why they are still playing today.

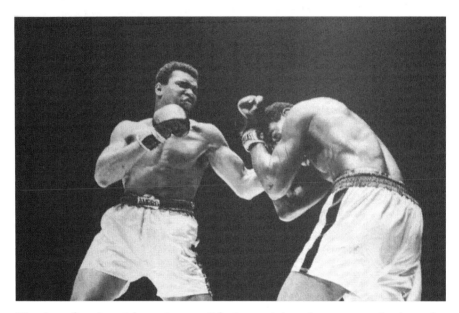

The lust for the girl made you lift the weights, but it was the love for the progress and development that kept you at the gym. For Steve Jobs: his ego. For Ali: a stolen bike. That's what got him into the gym, but is that what kept him going into the ring after taking hit after hit? Is that what got him up the next day with a broken nose, sore ribs, and two black eyes to train again for his next fight? Not at all.

Muhammad Ali found his WHY.

And that was to be the greatest boxer to ever step in the ring. You have to find your why for doing whatever it is in life you want to do. Because long after the initial lust or desire wears off, there has to be something that keeps you grinding away at it day in and day out. And that's when love comes into the picture.

"Take up one idea. Make that one idea your life - think of it, dream of it, live on that idea. Let the brain, muscles, nerves, every part of your body, be full of that idea, and just leave every other idea alone. This is the way to success."
-Swami Vivekananda

LUST

WHAT ARE 3 THINGS YOU TRULY DESIRE?

1. _____
2. _____
3. _____

WHAT ARE THE TOP 3 REASONS THAT YOU WANT TO ACHIEVE #1?

1. _____
2. _____
3. _____

WHAT ARE 3 THINGS THAT YOU DO EVERY DAY TO GET YOU CLOSER TO ACHIEVING #1?

1. _____
2. _____
3. _____

ONCE YOU ACHIEVE ONE OF YOUR TOP 3, HOW DO YOU SEE THIS IMPACTING YOUR LIFE? DO YOU THINK YOU WILL BE HAPPY? WHY?

_____

_____

NOTE:

IF YOU ACHIEVE WHAT YOU ARE WORKING SO HARD TOWARDS, BUT IT DOESN'T REALLY IMPACT YOUR LIFE OR MAKE YOU FEEL HOW YOU THOUGHT IT WOULD. IS IT REALLY WHAT YOU WANTED? IF YOU CAN'T ANSWER THAT QUESTION OR DON'T SEE IT IMPACTING YOUR LIFE OR MOOD IN A SIGNIFICANT WAY, THEN IT MIGHT BE SOMETHING ELSE YOU ARE REALLY CHASING.

IF YOUR GOAL IS TO MAKE IT TO THE NFL, BUT ONCE YOU GET THERE YOU'RE STILL NOT HAPPY. IT MIGHT BE THAT SUCCESS IS WHAT YOU ARE TRULY AFTER. OR MAYBE IT WAS MONEY THAT MOTIVATED YOU TO GET THERE AND ONCE YOU FOUND FINANCIAL SECURITY YOU REALIZED YOU WEREN'T IN LOVE WITH PLAYING FOOTBALL ANYMORE. MAYBE YOU ACTUALLY WANTED TO START YOUR OWN BUSINESS. THERE ARE MANY UNDERLYING MOTIVATORS FOR EACH PERSON AND THEY ARE NEVER PARTICULARLY SET IN STONE. THEY CAN COME AND GO AND REAPPEAR JUST LIKE SEASONS IN A YEAR.

BALANCE

ACCOUNTABILITY

LUST

LOVE

SACRIFICE

Love

To become a man, you must first understand that LOVE is much more than an emotion; it is an action. Love is about others—doing things to fulfill the needs of others, and taking care of their needs over your own. If you do this unselfishly, it comes back to you ten-fold. A man shows clearly what he truly loves.

The total athlete must be sound in body, mind, and spirit. If your spirit is off balance or needs something more, you will try and fill that void with other things. Family, beliefs, values, friends, your passion—these are all things that need to occupy space in your spirit in order for you to feel complete.

Spend your energy loving these things, giving your absolute attention to these things, and watch how it translates into your sport.

Lust can be the driving force that gets you moving towards a goal, but it is love that keeps you going. Often there isn't anything left in the tank, or whatever first motivated you to do something isn't there anymore.

You need to focus on your *WHY* to get through the times when nothing seems to be laid out in front of you. The love for your sport is what keeps you playing when perhaps the reason you started was something superficial. For your parents, the love for their family gets them up for work.

Your *WHY* will be your fuel. Own that and latch onto it.

"The first thing is to love your sport. Never do it to please someone else. It has to be yours."
- Peggy Fleming

.

There is no greater worldly love than that of a mother to a child. I am thankful to have the most amazing mother in the world, but it is my father's love that reminds me what it means to be a man. As a firefighter he worked long and difficult hours. It wasn't just the time on the job, but also the toll on his mind and body that was hard. This line of work may have some glory moments—pulling a cat down from a tree, a kid out of a burning building, or even the gift of delivering a baby on the way to the hospital.

I've heard hundreds of hero stories from his experiences, and even had the chance to witness many of them. But he often came home with the "Captain's Badge" still on his chest regardless if the uniform was off. I hated when he yelled at me like I was one of his subordinates, but then there were the moments when he came home from a shift and the first thing he did was grab me and give me a bear hug. It was like the weight of the world lifting off his chest (though I knew he could carry it if he had to).

In those moments I learned what love is all about.

He was just up on his feet for over 48 hours saving people's lives, and the only thing he cared about was spending some time with me. He could have easily gone straight to rest and not deal with anything, but he didn't. He dealt with me.

In your darkest times you need to Man Up. And after a hard day when things don't go your way, it will tell the true story of who you are as a Man.

"Obstacles don't have to stop you. If you run into a wall, don't turn around and give up. Figure out how to climb it, go through it, or work around it."
- Michael Jordan

The first basketball game I ever attended was Miami Heat vs. the Chicago Bulls. My father took me to the game. He wanted me to see who he thought was going to be one of the greatest players of our generation. He was certainly right about that. As much as I was a fan of sports, I was even more a student of the game.

So I watched everything, from the players talking trash, to the coach's reaction to the refs. But the one thing I noticed the most was the look in Michael Jordan's eyes when he had an opposing player beat. He would toy with him all night and get in his head. You could just see the love he had for the game. From that day forward I followed Jordan's career and spent more time watching the mind games he played than the incredible athleticism he displayed on the court. Needless to say from that day forward I was a Jordan fan through and through.

I remember June 16, 1996 like it was yesterday.

It was Father's Day, and Michael Jordan lay on the court in tears clutching a basketball to his chest. The Bulls just won the fourth of their six NBA Championships with an 87-75 victory against the Seattle Supersonics. Jordan wasn't crying because they won another championship or because he was 33 and scored a team-high of 22 points. It certainly wasn't because he was the league's Most Valuable Player during the season and in the finals. It was because this game, this whole season, was dedicated to his father.

Three years earlier Michael won his third NBA Final in a row with the Chicago Bulls. Jordan was considering walking away from the game; a fact no one but his father, James, knew. He and his father were extremely close and he had been there for every one of Michael's accomplishments from a young boy to a professional athlete. So, it was only natural that Michael confided in him about everything.

Michael and his father shared long conversations on the possibility of an early retirement. He felt like there wasn't anything left for basketball to give him. He couldn't find the passion he once had for the game, and he felt that without the passion driving him forward he would lose his gift. Yet, the inner turmoil he was feeling about the game didn't come even close to what he would feel in the coming months.

His father was found murdered in his car on the side of a North Carolina highway.

In Jordan's eyes, this was the final sign that it was his time to step away from basketball. Just as fast as he fell in love with the game, he fell out of it by losing the very person that was the glue holding it all together. That next year he played baseball for the Chicago White Sox in the MLB, chasing another dream that he and his father shared. With a year of media frenzy and not much success on the field—at least in Michael Jordan standards—he decided to return to basketball.

This time, with a newfound determination, he set out to win that year's NBA Finals for his father. Once he accomplished his goal, the pain, anguish, accomplishment and emotions he felt for his father all came out right there on center court.

It is clear that Michael Jordan loved his father deeply. If it wasn't for the shared love they had for the game, he probably wouldn't have worked so hard to get where he was in the first place. Then when Michael started to lose his passion for basketball (or his lust), it was the love he and his father shared that kept him practicing and playing day in and day out.

That's what it is really all about. Lust is the thing that you are reaching for; what you're chasing, that's the passion. But the *why* comes from the love that justifies what you're chasing through thick and thin.

For Michael Jordan, this was the bond that he and his father shared over the game of basketball. Michael didn't fall out of love with basketball: he momentarily lost his passion for the game, as many of us do in our own lives, relationships, sports, etc. There should always be a deep rooted foundation of why you are trying to accomplish something, why you are going through this journey. And it takes being a man to internalize those feelings and figure out what keeps you going even when the passion may be temporarily lost.

"There may be people that have more talent than you, but there's no excuse for anyone to work harder than you do."
- Derek Jeter

LOVE

WHAT ARE THE 5 THINGS YOU ARE MOST THANKFUL FOR?

1. _____

2. _____

3. _____

4. _____

5. _____

THINK BACK TO YOUR LIST OF WHAT YOU WERE PASSIONATE ABOUT. IF YOU WERE TO MOMENTARILY LOSE THOSE PASSIONS, WHAT ARE 3 THINGS YOU WOULD USE TO FUEL YOUR MOTIVATION?

1. _____

2. _____

3. _____

IF YOU WERE TO GET INDUCTED INTO THE HALL OF FAME, WHAT ARE 3 THINGS YOU WOULD WANT PEOPLE TO SAY ABOUT YOU?

1. _____

2. _____

3. _____

ASIDE FROM YOU SPORT. WHAT ARE 3 THINGS YOU FILL YOUR SPIRIT WITH?

1. _____

2. _____

3. _____

NOTE:

THE LIST OF THINGS YOU'VE LISTED ON THIS PAGE SHOULD MAKE YOU FEEL WHOLE. IT COULD BE PRAYING, OR BEING WITH FAMILY. IT COULD BE SPENDING TIME IN NATURE. BUT YOU MUST BE ABLE TO IDENTIFY WHAT MAKES YOU FEEL GOOD AS A PERSON OUTSIDE OF SPORTS. THERE WILL COME A DAY WHERE THE GAME IS NOT THERE FOR YOU ANYMORE. HOPEFULLY THAT IS A LONG TIME FROM NOW. BUT THE SOONER WE LOOK INTO OUR SOUL AND RECOGNIZE THE FUEL THAT IT NEEDS TO BE ABUNDANT, THE SOONER YOU WILL BECOME A MORE COMPLETE PERSON. AND THAT WILL TRANSFER INTO YOU BEING A MORE COMPLETE ATHLETE. THAT I PROMISE.

BALANCE

ACCOUNTABILITY

LUST

LOVE

SACRIFICE

Sacrifice

"Everything in life has a price; you have to decide whether the price is worth the prize."
-Coach Kav

The last and arguably most important step in manning up is SACRIFICE. You have heard you must make sacrifices to become great. But what does this actually mean? What things should you be sacrificing, and what things should you not be sacrificing in order to be a man?

If you are a high school athlete, I assume that your end goal is to play at the collegiate, and maybe even professional level, at some point in your career. If your goal at the moment is to play college ball, good for you.

But let me convince you to dream bigger.

There's nothing more gratifying than earning a scholarship or a roster spot on a college team, no matter what level. But what happens when you get there? Are you going to be complacent with where you are? I hope not! Remember, we should all work to be the greatest ever. If people aren't laughing at your goals, your goals are too small.

With that said, you have to realize the journey you are on is a long-term commitment. Playing a professional sport is no small feat. This is where sacrifice starts coming into play.

Remember my priorities as an athlete in regards to balance? God, Family, School, Sports. I also mentioned I took anything trying to come in between those things as a direct attack on my end goal as an athlete.

You must give up the distractions, because the goal is greater than whatever that short term interest may be.

I hated every minute of training, but I said, "Don't quit. Suffer now and live the rest of your life as a champion."
-Muhammad Ali

Kobe Bryant exemplifies the sacrifice and work ethic it takes to achieve greatness. Never mind his accolades; the sheer effort and determination he put into his craft is worthy of being in any book.

One of my favorite stories comes from a trainer (who requested to remain nameless) about his time helping Team USA with their conditioning prior to the Olympics. He recalled that on the night before the team's first scrimmage, he was lying on his bed half asleep when, around 4:15 a.m., his cell phone rang. It was Kobe.

"Hey [man], I hope I'm not disturbing anything right?"

"Uhh no, what's up Kobe?"

"Just wondering if you could just help me out with some conditioning work, that's all."

He checked his clock. 4:15 a.m.

"Yeah sure, I'll see you in the facility in a bit."

It took him about twenty minutes to get his gear and get out of the hotel. When he arrived and opened the room to the main practice floor, he saw Kobe. Alone. Drenched in sweat as if he had just taken a swim. It wasn't even 5:00 a.m.

They did some conditioning work for the next hour and fifteen minutes, then hit the weight room where they lifted for the another forty-five minutes. After that, they parted ways, and Kobe went back to the practice floor to shoot. The trainer came back around 11:00 a.m. when the scrimmage was scheduled to start. He saw Kobe among the other players, and asked what time Kobe finished up.

"Finish what?" Kobe replied.

"Getting your shots up. What time did you leave?"

"Oh just now. I wanted 800 makes so yeah, just now."

There wasn't anyone in the world that was willing to outwork Kobe Bryant. His play showed for it well into the late part of his thirties.

"People do not differ in their desire to win; they differ in the price they are willing to pay to win."
-Unknown

Sacrifices don't just come in the form of conditioning and shooting a thousand shots at 5 o'clock in the morning.

Sometimes you may want to sacrifice your morals and what you know is right in order to try and get a leg up. It may seem like the shortcut you're taking today will get you to your goal faster, but the reality is the shortcut will end up taking you on the long road to your end goal.

The case of Barry Bonds can be considered a negative case of both lust and sacrifice. Throughout the 1990s, Bonds was one of the best players in baseball because of his all-around talent. But that wasn't enough for him. He wanted more.

In the book *Game of Shadows*, authors Mark Fainaru-Wada and Lance Williams dug deep into the notorious BALCO steroids scandal and Bonds' use of performance enhancing drugs. One of the reasons given in the book for Bonds' use of steroids was his jealousy towards Mark McGwire, who hit a then-record of 70 home runs in 1998.

Bonds knew McGwire wasn't clean and was pissed off that Big Mac was stealing all of the headlines. Bonds became obsessed with that record and was going to do whatever it took to show the world that he was the best. Taking steroids led to Bonds reaching all of his goals. He set the single-season home run record with 73 blasts in 2001 at 36 years old.

From 2001-2004, he made what is arguably one of the hardest things to do in professional sports — hitting a baseball — look easy. His numbers would have been impressive on a slo-pitch softball team and he retired as the all-time leader in home runs with 762.

However, it came with a hefty price. All of those gaudy stats he acquired with steroids now have an asterisk next to them.

He was always known for his rude and abrasive attitude, but, before he took the juice, at least nobody could doubt his baseball ability. He was a no-doubt, first-ballot Hall of Famer before he cheated. It wasn't up for debate. Now, he might not even get in. The story of Roger Clemens is similar. He has to live with this for the rest of his life.

This story is the perfect example of how trying to take a shortcut to achieve your goal faster can ultimately derail you from your goal. Bonds' shortcut knocked him out of the Hall of Fame in the sport he'd been working on his whole life. Temptations and distractions are not going to do anything but hinder you on your journey to success. The smart sacrifices you make today are the real shortcuts to your long term goals.

"Today I will do what others won't, so tomorrow I can accomplish what others can't."
-Jerry Rice

No matter how hard anyone works, the ultimate form of sacrifice was from Jesus. This was indeed the greatest act of sacrifice in the history of the world. He freely laid His life down for you and me. Therefore, all thanks, praise and honor should go directly to Him!

Jesus said in John 15:13 that there is "**No greater love that a man can have than this: that he lay his life down for his friends!**"

When you know your passion and your drive—your *why*—you are less likely to be distracted by the shiny objects in front of you. When you are prioritizing you must have focus. If you don't, you will find the wrong things to fill the gap. If your main focus is to be a professional athlete, but you also say, "Oh, I need to go make money too." then you aren't putting the sacrifices in front of your goal. You're not one-tracking your mind to only worry about one outcome. The shiny object will be your focus instead of the end-goal you want so desperately to achieve.

"And do not forget to do good and to share with others, for with such sacrifices God is pleased"
-Hebrews 13:16

SACRIFICE

WHAT IS THE BIGGEST REGRET YOU HAVE IN YOUR SPORTS CAREER SO FAR?

_____
_____
_____

WHAT COULD YOU HAVE SACRIFICED IN ORDER TO KEEP THAT FROM TURNING INTO A REGRET?

_____
_____
_____

WHAT ARE 3 SACRIFICES YOU ARE MAKING RIGHT NOW TO GET YOU CLOSER TO YOUR GOAL?

1. _____

2. _____

3. _____

WHAT ARE 3 NEW THINGS YOU COULD START SACRIFICING IN ORDER TO GET YOU CLOSER TO YOUR GOAL?

1. _____

2. _____

3. _____

WHAT IS THE EXCUSE YOU USE MOST OFTEN IN YOUR LIFE?

_____

_____

_____

The KEY to Success

I grew up playing cards with my father and his crew in Miami. We played many games, but poker stood out the most. I learned to hold 'em, fold 'em, how to bluff, how to read other players to see if they were bluffing, and how to raise the stakes without letting everyone know I had a good hand. It took me a while to grasp the concepts, but once I did I couldn't believe how applicable the game was to dealing with people in real life.

I think my father knew this, and that's why he let me sit in on the games as a youngster. I've taken those learned lessons with me, and I apply a lot of them to how I deal with people today.

While in office, Harry Truman kept a sign on his desk that read, "The Buck Stops Here."

You may or may not have heard the saying "pass the buck". This phrase dates back to the old western days. It's likely something your parents or grandparents say, but at the time a buck knife was used to tell who was to deal the next deck of cards. If someone didn't want to deal, he could "pass the buck".

If you slept through American History, Harry Truman became the 33rd president of the United States following Franklin Roosevelt's death in 1945. Truman's decision to drop the atomic bombs on Japan in the first few months of his presidency ultimately ended WWII. His meaning behind the sign on his desk was no matter how many people along the chain of command leading to his office avoided taking responsibility or blame for something, he would take the burden.

The concept of taking ownership in action is extremely important when becoming the leader and controller of your own future success. Truman was quoted saying, "The president—whoever he may be—has to decide. He can't pass the buck to anybody. No one else can do the deciding for him. That's his job."

Responsibility weighs the heaviest on leaders.

The higher the leader (player, captain, coach), the heavier the responsibility. As president, Truman carried the weight of the entire nation (and arguably the world) on his shoulders during WWII. Leaders may give up many things and delegate to others, but the one thing the top leader can never let go of is final responsibility.

You have to be the "president" of your own life. That's what manning up is all about. Take responsibility for everything that happens in your life and in your sport. If you stop passing the buck on to someone else, stop making excuses, and take action to fix a problem and become a better you, you will see your life change right in front of your eyes.

Ultimately you will transform into a man.

I don't know if I've found the key to success in life, although I think I've found what works for me. What I do know is the key to athletic success is your understanding of what I mean when explaining the KEYs:

First and foremost you must have the *Knowledge*.

What I mean is knowing exactly what you want to accomplish, what it takes to get you there, and knowing the plan to that point. This comes from observing—being a student of the game and the process. Observe and study other successful people. Watch those who are already where you want to be. There's a reason that I used successful people as examples. We learn from those that have been through what we are trying to accomplish. Whether that's through good or bad outcomes, we must be willing to watch, listen, and learn in order to replicate their success and overcome their failures.

Secondly you must *Execute*.

You're going to take your knowledge and deploy a strategy you planned, but now you're going to take action. When you begin to take action, you will learn what works and what does not. When you fail, you are going to fail fast. There's nothing wrong with failing; we learn more from our mistakes than from our triumphs. Trust me: before any success and achievement in your life you are going to have multiple failures. I always tell my athletes that in order to master something you must have at least 3 peaks and 2 valleys. What I mean is that in order to be the best at something or be considered a master at a skill, you must have at least 2 failures. The end goal is the third peak. You have to brush yourself off after each failure, and climb your way back up. So, in deploying the KEYs you must first create and gain the knowledge of what it is you want, and what you have to do to get there. Then you need to develop a strategy and be able to execute it. We can plan and plan all our life but if we never take the initiative and execute, nothing will ever come of our efforts. Your strategy will not be perfect at first, but trust in the process, adjust when needed, and make sure you see it out to the end.

The third and final component to the KEYs is realizing the only thing that's going to be the X-factor in this whole process is *You*.

You have to gain the knowledge yourself, you have to execute, and you have to be the one that mans up and takes responsibility for everything you do. If you don't really want it, or don't want to really work for it and own the process, then I promise no amount of planning or half-ass executing is going to get you to the top. The fire must live inside of you. If you want something, or see someone successful and say, "I want to be like that person," but you aren't willing to make sacrifices and put in the work to get to that point, I question if you really truly want it, or if you just think you would like to be in that person's shoes. There's a big difference between wanting to be like Lebron James and wanting to put in all the work and make all the sacrifices he has made to be one of the best basketball players ever.

In the end it's on you. I can tell you what it means to MAN UP. I can tell you what it means to Grow Some BALLS. I can even outline the

KEYs to athletic success. What I can't do is the work for you. You have to take the initiative in your life and in your sport.

It's up to you to MAN UP.

About the Author:

Justin Kavanaugh is the founder and CEO of The Sport and Speed Institute. A company dedicated to "Empowering America's Athletes." He has worked with over 50,000 athletes and helped over 850 of them recruited into college.

Coach Kav has over 15 years of coaching experience. His facility and training methods provide his athletes with the highest quality coaching, personalized services, and the relationships needed for them to reach their fullest potential. He knows exactly what it takes to reach the highest levels of sports performance. He's developed athletes starting in middle school and guided them all the way to reaching their dream of playing in the pro's.

His mentorship and guidance in not only their sport but in his athlete's personal lives is the reason for his continued success. Coach Kavanaugh's mission is to teach valuable lessons and foster lasting relationships with his athletes that last beyond their days on the playing field.

Made in the USA
San Bernardino, CA
12 October 2017